I0424420

SPEAK SOFTLY …

SPEAK SOFTLY ...

♦

WHAT'S HAPPENED TO AMERICAN HUMILITY?

Ira L. Williams, III

iUniverse, Inc.
New York Lincoln Shanghai

SPEAK SOFTLY ...
WHAT'S HAPPENED TO AMERICAN HUMILITY?

Copyright © 2007 by Debut Ventures, Inc.

All rights reserved. No part of this book may be used or reproduced by any means, graphic, electronic, or mechanical, including photocopying, recording, taping or by any information storage retrieval system without the written permission of the publisher except in the case of brief quotations embodied in critical articles and reviews.

iUniverse books may be ordered through booksellers or by contacting:

iUniverse
2021 Pine Lake Road, Suite 100
Lincoln, NE 68512
www.iuniverse.com
1-800-Authors (1-800-288-4677)

The views expressed in this work are solely those of the author and do not necessarily reflect the views of the publisher, and the publisher hereby disclaims any responsibility for them.

ISBN: 978-0-595-42787-1 (pbk)
ISBN: 978-0-595-68187-7 (cloth)
ISBN: 978-0-595-87119-3 (ebk)

Printed in the United States of America

Contents

Author's Note 1

Preface 5

The Premise 9

In this book we will: 15

Defining Humility 19

Humility and the Founders 23

Lincoln's Humility 31

America in the 20th Century 35

Humble Heroes 39

Where Did We Get Off-track? 43

How Can We Be Humble and Powerful? 51

21st-century Humility 63

Humility and Pride 71

How Do We Bring Back Humility? 75

What About Carrying the Big Stick? 93

Endnotes 97

Author's Note

Initially I had planned to pen some lofty language that conveyed the gratitude, reverence and appreciation I have for all of those individuals who directly or indirectly impacted the writing of this book. In the end, though, I thought that it would be so much more effective to provide each of you with a direct and personal tribute.

My Lord, Jesus—For motivation and direction. Without a doubt, the words on these pages would not exist without your stirring in my soul on the Animas River in Colorado. I pray that this project fulfills your will.

Carmen—You continue to be the living manifestation of God's grace. Each day, I thank Him that you and I are together, because I've done nothing to deserve such a perfect wife. I love you!

Gabrielle and T.J.—What little pride I intentionally stoke in my heart is directed at you two. Your gifts are many, and we all know what that means. (Remember Luke 12:48.) I thank you for spurring me to be the best Dad I can be.

My mother, Jackie—For planting in me the love of reading and writing. And for reminding me that I can do anything I put my mind to. (I know I can swim. I know I can swim. I know I can swim.…)

My father, Ira II—For daring me to be audacious. Whether I was running for student government posts, applying to those "stretch" schools, buying real estate at 21, or courting (then marrying) a woman who lived 2,000 miles away, you've always encouraged me to play big. Why stop now?

Corey, Millicent, Earl, Oneka, and Darian—Our friendship has been a deep reservoir of strength for me. You have each reminded me that this has been an exercise in persistence and a walk of faith. And with you in my corner, I knew that failure was not an option!

Kenneth Ulmer, Tom Mullins, John Maxwell, Rob Koke, Beth Moore, John Bevere, and Rob Bell—Each of you has shown me how to be an unabashed Christ follower and passionate man of God in the 21st century. Some of you have been my pastors, others I have admired from afar. Your teachings are intelligent and informed, your writings are relevant and radical. All of which provide the template that I pray I will follow for years to come.

<u>Seth Godin</u>—For over ten years, I've been watching and learning from you. Your introduction to the world of publishing (both traditional and non) has been incredibly influential. Oh, and the callouts about "Speak Softly ..." on your blog haven't hurt either.

<u>Michael Dell</u>—Having the opportunity to see first-hand what a Level 5 leader looks like has been a unique privilege. Knowing that you've developed these capabilities on the job over the last 23 years is all the more impressive. You are clearly comfortable in your own skin as a person and as a leader. That comfort (and resulting humility) is something for which all of us should strive.

<u>Last, but certainly not least, Ms. Jenny Meadows</u>—Who would have imagined that a simple Google search would lead me to the perfect editor/proofreader/grammarian and writing coach? Thank you for pushing me when you knew I needed it, and validating this work from Day One.

I thank you all for encouraging me in this endeavor.

Preface

I'm fully aware of the paradox of trying to make an impassioned exhortation ... about humility. How do I shout from the rooftops that it's time for us to speak softly?

The reality is that it's hard to be perceived as both humble and assertive.

Just ask Moses.

In the Book of Numbers, Chapter 12, Verse 3, it says, "Now Moses was a very humble man, more humble than anyone else on the face of the earth."

While this was no doubt true, we can't ignore the fact that Moses himself wrote the book of Numbers!

Moses, however, was a better man than I, and was far better equipped to be a humble servant/leader. I'll do my best to strike that same balance in the tone and content of this book.

I'm also aware that mine are beliefs and opinions that might seem, at best, out of step with the 21st-century American public. At worst, this project could be written off as a naïve, overly simplified ode to mediocrity.

Moreover, I'm not a professional writer. I'm not a social scientist. I'm not a trained researcher. At best, I'm a pretty good student of history, with a decent ability to recognize patterns and communicate abstract ideas to others.

So, from that perspective, I clearly have plenty to be humble about as I approach this project.

Undaunted, I am moving forward with this book because I believe that our loss of humility is at the root of many social challenges we face.

But please be clear on this: I'm optimistic about our prospects.

I don't think it will be that hard to recalibrate ourselves to embrace humility. I think we need only revert to some of the underlying beliefs and values that Americans have traditionally held dear.

For me, my Christian faith provides a perfect framework for this study of humility. Jesus lived a humble life. He walked the talk. Throughout history, other men and women of faith did so as well.

From the Apostle Paul, St. Augustine, and Joan of Arc, to John Wesley, Dr. Martin Luther King Jr., and Mother Teresa, we have plenty of role models who led strong yet humble lives.

I also appreciate that not everyone shares my faith. I hope, though, to provide sufficient evidence and support to persuade all readers, regardless of their beliefs.

I won't try to hide from or dance around the role that I believe faith plays in humility. If faith is defined as *the substance of things hoped for, the evidence of things not seen* (Hebrews 11:1), then those with faith are acknowledging that they are not in control of their own existence.

Those of us with an active faith have already humbled ourselves to the extent that we know that God is directing our actions. Further, to remain in His will, we need to remain humble and others-oriented in our thoughts and actions.

Thus, my intent is to offer a compelling case, supported by data and anecdotes from an eclectic collection of sources, that proves my premise: that humility is the cornerstone of a fulfilling, satisfying and purposeful life.

The Premise

Humility is an old-fashioned word. It brings to mind images of hunched shoulders, bowed heads, whispered voices. It makes us think of weakness.

It makes us think of individuals afraid to speak up for themselves. It is almost a condescending term given to people who have forsaken their own needs and desires in order to serve others. "He's such a sweet, humble man …" or "She is so humble and unassuming.…"

What goes unspoken, though, is that we would never trade places with that sweet, humble man or that humble, unassuming woman.

It's human nature to want one's own interests served. Altruism is a learned trait. From the time we are children, we are taught and conditioned to know that, in order to get along with other kids in the sandbox, we have to share. We can't snatch things from others.

And, absolutely no biting.

Thus, as we get older and leave the playground behind, we get to a place where we are not nearly as selfish as we were as children. However, we still tend to be self-*oriented*.

We often look inward to ask ourselves, "What would make me happy? What do I need? How can my life be improved?"

As Americans, we have a deeply rooted sense of individualism that is at the heart of our unprecedented rise to power in less than 250 years of existence. The inalienable rights described in the Declaration of Independence have empowered Americans to approach their lives with unfettered optimism that there is little that can stand in the way of their "pursuit of happiness."

As a result, our perspective on the outside world, for better or worse, tends to be informed by its impact on us.

How do the policies of my government affect my day-to-day life?

How does the performance of my company affect my paycheck?

How well is my school district preparing my kids for college?

Why does it cost so much to put gas in my car?

This is not to say that we, as a nation, are completely self-absorbed and blind to the needs of others. We have a long history of generosity that continues to this day. We send billions of dollars in aid around the world to help relieve the suffering of others.

The generosity of Americans is not in question.

The humility of Americans is.

Remember, for most of us, humility is equated with weakness. Americans are repelled by weakness of any sort. We crave strength because strength facilitates success, and success is believed to be key to our pursuit of happiness.

I submit, however, that it requires tremendous strength and character to place others' needs before your own.

I believe that by moving our self-orientation to the background and truly focusing upon enhancing the lives of those around us, we can not only attain a more balanced perspective on the world, but we can also find greater personal fulfillment for ourselves.

Because here's the secret: In order to be humble, you have to be strong. And you have to be so comfortable with that strength that you don't need to flaunt it.

Moreover, the truly humble know that they have an obligation to reach out to and serve those who are weaker than they are. The best historical example of this juxtaposition of humility and strength is Jesus Christ.

As the Son of God, he clearly had all the power he needed. Yet throughout his earthly life, he served others. He ministered to the downtrodden. He even washed his followers' feet![1]

Now, I know I lost some of you there, but I hope you didn't miss the message.

With true power comes an obligation to wield that power with humility and a lack of arrogance.

It would be an understatement to say that we, as Americans, have lost sight of the merits of humility.

In describing his vision of the ideal American foreign policy, 2000 presidential candidate Gov. George W. Bush put it this way:

If we're an arrogant nation, they'll resent us; if we're a humble nation, but strong, they'll welcome us. And our nation stands alone right now in the world in terms of power, and that's why we've got to be humble, and yet project strength in a way that promotes freedom.[2]

Admirable as that vision was, we cannot avoid the fact that, right or wrong, our reputation with friends and foes around the world is anything but humble.

That said, I want to focus on the role of humility in our day-to-day lives, and point out how we have gotten away from a core American value.

In this book we will:

- Review the admirable American tradition of humility and try to identify where we lost the trail

- Spotlight the harm caused by a lack of humility in our interpersonal relationships

- Identify nine specific steps we can all take to improve our interpersonal relationships by adopting an attitude of humility

My hope is that this book will spur a new type of self-examination. We must understand that humility is woven into the fabric of America, and that our society would be well served by a more humble attitude in all of our interactions.

Our strength as a nation is rooted in the humility of the giants of our past. Washington. Jefferson. Adams. Franklin. Lincoln.

Roosevelt. All were dominant figures in our history, and all demonstrated the balance between strength and humility.

I also believe that those willing to entertain the notion that strength comes from humility will find that their perspective on the world around them will change for the better.

Many of us are burdened by an inflated sense of our own self-worth. As a result, we often find ourselves driven to convince those around us of our importance while striving for unachievable levels of self-serving success. However, once we appreciate that we are relatively insignificant players in the machinations of this world, we can embrace a more balanced blend of happiness and accomplishment.

We can then begin to acknowledge the personal fulfillment we gain by re-directing our energies.

I intend to focus on the role of humility in the lives of everyday Americans. It is my firm belief that by adopting a more humble perspective as a nation, we will not only find that our relationships with others improve, but our reputation as a nation improves.

The title of this book is taken from a West African proverb made famous by President Theodore Roosevelt.

The entire proverb reads, "Speak softly and carry a big stick; you will go far."[3]

The "big stick" line is the one that often gets the focus. Everyone likes the idea of being able to get the results we desire, even (or especially) if that means we have to get tough to do so.

(Arguably that was President Roosevelt's intent when recalling the proverb, given his preference for forward-leaning domestic and foreign policies.)

I re-read the proverb, though, and considered how widely known and embraced it is by Americans. And it became clear that this is a microcosmic statement summing up the role America has to fulfill in the 21st century.

Most importantly, if we look at the proverb in its entirety, we understand that it is a statement advising balance. It won't be enough to simply carry a big stick. That smacks of arrogance, and that attitude will be resisted everywhere.

We must re-learn ways to speak softly, and truly project humility to our neighbors, comfortable that it will not be forgotten that we are wielders of unprecedented strength.

And only with that balance will we "go far" as individuals and as a nation.

Defining Humility

Let's start off with a definition of the word *humility*.

Most dictionaries use some variation of the following definition:

> *The quality or condition of being humble.*

OK, so what does it mean to be humble?

One definition of humble is *marked by meekness or modesty in behavior, attitude, or spirit; not arrogant or prideful.*

Modesty. Not arrogant or prideful. Both of those make sense.

But what about this idea of meekness? That sounds like weakness.

Well, meek is defined as *showing patience; gentle.*

So being humble is being modest. Patient. Gentle. Not arrogant or prideful.

While all of this is true, please allow me to add some additional color and context to these dictionary definitions.

For our purposes, humility will be defined as:

> *The willingness to consider the needs and desires of others before your own.*

Humility is having the confidence and comfort in knowing that it is infinitely more satisfying to focus on enhancing the lives of others than trying to achieve one's own fulfillment.

At least if we set as a goal to make someone else's existence a bit more pleasant, we have a good chance at success.

Is humility a permanent trait? No, for most mortals like us, it is, at best, a periodic personality attribute.

In classic terms, to be humble is to be deferential, respectful, contrite, acquiescent, self-effacing.

In today's vernacular, being humble is knowing that it's not always about you.

What you'll notice is that, while each definition shades the term *humble* in a slightly different fashion, what it never connotes is weakness. Reserved? Yes. Even subservient, perhaps.

But what we must realize is that simply by considering our own interests as secondary to those of others, we are not weakened. Our own worth is not diminished by celebrating and elevating that of our neighbor.

I will make a point of including pertinent quotations about humility throughout this text. And one of my favorite addresses this relationship between humility and self-worth.

Humility does not mean thinking less of yourself than of other people, nor does it mean having a low opinion of your own gifts. It means freedom from thinking about yourself at all.[4]

That's the real gift of humility: it frees us to think about others and how to touch their lives in a positive manner.

With this behind us, let's explore the way that humility has been woven into the American fabric from the very beginning.

Humility and the Founders

Humility has historically been a prominent element of the American ethos.

A quick review of some of the writings of the Founding Fathers makes it clear that many of them believed that the ultimate success of this new nation would depend in part on the willingness of its citizens and its leaders to consider the needs of the nation above their own desires.

For many, like George Washington and John Adams, this embracing of humility was rooted in their Christian faith. In his letter to the governors of the 13 states at the time of his retirement from command of the Continental Army, Washington prays that God will protect the governors and their states.

He also asks that God would *incline the hearts of the citizens to culti-vate a spirit of subordination and obedience to government, to entertain a brotherly affection and love for one another, for their fellow-citizens of the United States at large, and particularly for brethren who have served in the Field ...* [5]

Using terms like *subordination* and *obedience to government* may cause us some degree of discomfort today. But I believe Washington and his contemporaries understood clearly that their then-experi-mental government depended completely on the willingness of the people to forgo some of their individual freedoms in order to enjoy the inalienable rights as defined in the Declaration of Independence.

Given that Washington was surely familiar with the Bible and its dozens of references to the virtues of humility, it's hard to imagine that he wouldn't expect the country to embrace a similar spirit. In fact, he concludes his prayer for the governors with the following petition:

... and finally that he would most graciously be pleased to dispose us all to do justice, to love mercy, and to demean ourselves with that charity, humility and pacific temper of mind, which were the characteristics of the Divine Author of our blessed religion, and without an humble imi-tation of whose example in these things, we can never hope to be a happy nation. [6]

If we have a problem with *subordination* then being asked to *demean ourselves* would be a deal breaker.

But, if we again put aside the semantic nuances and appreciate his intended message, Washington's words are far more palatable: we need to temper our own personal drives and desires with charity and humility (that is, become others-oriented). Otherwise, Washington warned us, our nation would never achieve its ambition of being a city upon a hill.

For John Adams, humility provided necessary safeguards against what he believed were man's natural tendencies toward selfishness. In his essay "Thoughts on Government," Adams proposed annual elections of public servants. He believed that:

This will teach them the great political virtues of humility, patience, and moderation, without which every man in power becomes a ravenous beast of prey.[7]

Adams was also adamant that selflessness and charity were key ingredients for the American character.

In a letter to his granddaughter in 1820, Adams echoed the instructions found in the Biblical book of Micah when he advises her to *Do justly. Love mercy. Walk humbly. This is enough.*[8]

Likewise, that same scripture seems to have prompted Adams, in 1756, to imagine:

... a nation in some distant region should take the Bible for their only law book, and every member should regulate his conduct by the precepts there exhibited! Every member would be obliged in conscience to tem-

perance, frugality, and industry; to justice, kindness, and charity towards his fellow man; and to piety, love, and reverence toward Almighty God.[9]

Once again, we see that charity toward our fellow citizens was deemed a highly desirable if not required attribute of Americans.

If Washington and Adams were driven by their faith to seek humility, then Jefferson and Franklin could be said to have been more pragmatic, if not calculating, in their acknowledgment that humility was a virtue.

Jefferson was a well-known proponent of the merits of logic and reason. But this rational worldview was still reliant upon a predisposition to consider the interests of others.

In his letter to Thomas Law in 1814, Jefferson actually asserts that morality itself is rooted in selflessness.

Self-interest, or rather self-love, or egoism, has been more plausibly substituted as the basis of morality. But I consider our relations with others as constituting the boundaries of morality. With ourselves, we stand on the ground of identity, not of relation, which … requiring two subjects, excludes self-love confined to a single one. To ourselves … we can owe no duties, obligation requiring also two parties. Self-love, therefore, is no part of morality. Indeed, it is exactly its opposite. [10]

In a letter to John Adams in 1816, Jefferson puts it more succinctly:

I believe ... that every human mind feels pleasure in doing good to another.[11]

To Jefferson, a well-balanced individual was someone who, in addition to having a burning desire for liberty, freedom and truth, would also be enhanced by assuming some of the "duties and obligations" of his/her fellow citizen.

Interestingly, as we Americans become more sophisticated, rational and informed (which Jefferson would applaud), we seem to have elevated self-interest to a place where Jefferson would likely disapprove. In a later chapter, we'll try to identify how that evolution took place.

Ben Franklin actually made the pursuit of humility one of his life-long goals. When he was a young man, he identified thirteen virtues that he would use as guiding principles in the way he lived his life.

One of those was humility, which he freely admitted was a challenge for him to truly achieve, but fairly easy for him to at least display.

I cannot boast of much success in acquiring the reality of this virtue, but I had a good deal with regard to the appearance of it.[12]

True to Franklin's wry and often self-deprecating manner, he also admitted that he was constantly at battle with his pride.

Even if I could conceive that I had completely overcome it, I would probably be proud of my humility.[13]

Franklin, more than the other founders discussed here, was one who freely acknowledged that humility (or at least the appearance of humility) could be useful as a social tool, enabling individuals to simply get along better.

Would you win the hearts of others, you must not seem to vie with them, but to admire them. Give them every opportunity of displaying their own qualifications, and when you have indulged their vanity, they will praise you in turn and prefer you above others … Such is the vanity of mankind that minding what others say is a much surer way of pleasing them than talking well ourselves.[14]

Cynical and self-serving though that might sound, it still provides a compelling reason for the adoption of an orientation toward others: we might simply get more done with less strife.

Washington, Adams, Jefferson and Franklin were clearly key players as architects of the American republic. They were also men whose beliefs and philosophies directly impacted their perceptions of what the nation would stand for, what its place in the world would be, and how its citizens would engage with one another.

What's important to note is that these men who are often thought of as die-hard freedom fighters and proponents of liberty each believed that for the nation to truly thrive, its citizens had to be steeped in humility, charity and selflessness.

We'll see that Abraham Lincoln took that same basic belief and wove it into his philosophies about domestic policy.

Lincoln's Humility

In the 80-plus years following the founding of the nation, America had experienced nearly unfettered growth and prosperity. Yet, the longstanding issue of slavery continued to fester until the Civil War broke out in July of 1861.

The following month, President Lincoln issued his famous proclamation of a day of fasting
... to be observed by the people of the United States with religious solemnities, and the offering of fervent supplications to Almighty God for the safety and welfare of these States, His blessings on their arms, and a speedy restoration of peace.[15]

This overtly spiritual rhetoric was not at all unusual for Lincoln, who made no secret of the importance of his faith in his life.

In this proclamation, Lincoln goes on to instruct his countrymen that it is appropriate for *all people, at all times, to acknowledge and revere the Supreme Government of God; to bow in humble submission to his chastisements ...,*[16] thus reminding Americans that even in this country where freedom and liberty had been such a source of national pride, there still needed to be an attitude of submission to God's will.

Even in 1861, there seemed to have been a realization that the United States had been blessed with vast potential for future prosperity. Lincoln keys on this fact, and points out that even a country as anointed as America must remain humble.

And whereas, when our own beloved country, once, by the blessing of God, united, prosperous, and happy, is now afflicted with faction and civil war, it is peculiarly fit for us to recognize the hand of God in this terrible visitation, and ... to humble ourselves before Him and to pray for His mercy ... [17]

A subtlety that should be pointed out about Lincoln's proclamation is that it was intended to be a *universal* day of prayer and meditation. He specifically makes the recommendation

... to all the People, and especially to all ministers and teachers of religion of all denominations, and to all heads of families to observe and keep that day, according to their several creeds and modes of worship, in all humility and with all religious solemnity ... [18]

Inclusive, others-oriented petitions, prayers and fasting from all citizens were what Lincoln sought.

This notion of humility in the face of great blessings was a recurring theme in Lincoln's public pronouncements. In 1863, in a proclamation for another national fast day, he drives home points that would be equally convicting today, let alone 140 years ago.

We have been the recipients of the choicest bounties of Heaven. We have been preserved, these many years, in peace and prosperity. We have grown in numbers, wealth, and power as no other nation has ever grown; but we have forgotten God. We have forgotten the gracious hand which preserved us in peace, and multiplied and enriched and strengthened us; and we have vainly imagined ... that all these blessings were produced by some superior wisdom and virtue of our own. Intoxicated with unbroken success, we have become too self-sufficient to feel the necessity of redeeming and preserving grace, too proud to pray to the God that made us. It behooves us, then, to humble ourselves before the offended Power, to confess our national sins, and to pray for clemency and forgiveness.[19]

In language far more articulate than I could ever muster, President Lincoln identifies the crux of a problem that we are still grappling with today: in the face of phenomenal national success, we have begun to believe our own press, we have become exceptionally self-oriented, and we have begun to replace humility with hubris.

What's intriguing, though, is that while Lincoln might have sensed this trend in the mid-19th century, we will see that in the subsequent four-score-and-seven-year period, the combination of world wars, economic cataclysm and social upheaval actually conspired to *increase* American humility in the first half of the 20th century.

America in the 20th Century

As America grew in global relevance in WWII, it was far from clear that this country would emerge from the war as a superpower.

America's reluctant entry into the hostilities in Europe and the fact that it required a humiliating surprise attack at Pearl Harbor to spur us into engagement in the Pacific were signs that this nation was not looking to throw its increasing weight around.

To the contrary, there was a more "workman-like" perspective about our role in the world at that time. The average American had an attitude that when we were called to do a job, we would do it, do it well, but without any undue fanfare.

To this day, the men and women of what we've come to refer to as "The Greatest Generation" are generally unwilling to assume that

"Greatest" mantle. Their comments about their call to duty are almost universally humble, with a consistent refrain of "just serving my country."

More specifically, these Americans came of age in a time of economic weakness, when few had any capacity for developing an over-sized sense of self-importance. To the contrary, life was humbling almost everyone, and the only things most Americans had to be proud of were their personal integrity and values.

That said, we were a people with an insatiable commitment to those values and beliefs (i.e., The American Way), and we would be willing to make whatever sacrifice to protect those beliefs.

But even as victors after WWII, we were gracious and reached out to lift up those we had just defeated. There was almost no gloating, no oppression, no retribution.

Americans grew into being perceived as a benevolent superpower because we were not flaunting our power in the faces of the weaker members of the world community. Instead, we were seen to be serving them and lifting them up.

The Marshall Plan was the most dramatic and impactful example of that post-war generosity.

Even today, it's tough to appreciate the unprecedented scope of the openhandedness demonstrated by the United States between 1948 and 1952. As the only participant in the European theatre that had not had its national infrastructure devastated, the US had an upper hand on almost any measure in relation to the rest of the West.

Rather than lord that over those countries, the US extended 16 European nations more than $13B in financial aid (all but $1.5B as grants, not loans). Not only did this gesture help the citizens avoid widespread starvation and abject poverty, it jumpstarted the economy of Europe. That period became the most economically productive era in European history, and helped to "permit the emergence of political and social conditions in which free institutions can exist." [20]

For all intents and purposes, the United States had delivered a knockout blow to its enemies in the war. But rather than kick them while they were down, we picked them up, brushed them off, and made them stronger and more self-sufficient than ever before.

Certainly there was strategic self-interest at work as well. But there's no denying that America passed up the opportunity to humiliate our former foes. Instead, we extended a helping hand out of generosity and selflessness.

Humble Heroes

Even as the entertainment and media industries grew in prominence in the 1930s through the 1950s, the widely accepted archetype of the American Hero was the brave, honorable and humble guy.

Jimmy Stewart made a career playing earnest, honest men with an unerring sense of right and wrong. But you never saw him blowing his own horn, demanding attention for himself, either onscreen or off. It just wasn't done that way.

The cowboy heroes of the silver screen were equally unwilling to seek recognition for their derring-do. In fact, I believe uttering the line "Aww shucks, ma'am" accompanied by a downward gaze and a boot kicking dirt must have been on page 1 of the "Silver Screen Cowboy Manual."

Even those heroes who were a bit more "flashy" in their execution went to great lengths not to attract lingering attention. The Lone Ranger would do what needed to be done, and then ride off into the sunset, leaving behind only a silver bullet as a calling card.

In the superhero domain, you had a host of comic book and television heroes who went so far as to adopt secret identities to avoid attention. None wanted to be publicly recognized for their heroism. It just wasn't done that way.

Even sports heroes were talented but modest men whose on-the-field demeanor was intentionally low-key. In striking contrast to today's sports heroes, these men thought it unprofessional to celebrate their personal successes on the field.

Look at old films of Jackie Robinson or Joe DiMaggio rounding the bases after a homerun. Head down, moving along diligently. No hopping, skipping, leaping and admiring the ball as it cleared the fence.

That would have been deeply frowned upon.

In fact, there was (and is) an unwritten code of conduct in baseball that warned against "showing up" a competitor. The repercussions could be directed at the offender or his teammate, and it would typically be in the form of a "message pitch" delivered at the soft tissue on his person.

In football, the message to young players tempted to celebrate a touchdown or other on-field success was to "act like you've been there before."

Jim Brown had more football talent than nearly anyone to play the game. Yet after his spectacular touchdown runs, he'd simply turn and hand the ball to an official. On the other side of the ball, Dick Butkus would deliver a devastating blow, then turn and walk back to his huddle.

(Of course Butkus might have some choice language for his unfortunate adversary, but that was in the heat of the battle and, most importantly, not for the benefit of the fans.)

What you wouldn't see Brown do is break into a full-fledged dance number after a touchdown. Butkus wouldn't rip off his helmet and mug for a TV camera after a sack. It just wasn't done that way.

They were acting like professionals. Like they had been there before.

Needless to say, this sense of understatement and humility by those in the public eye is a thing of the past. There is clearly a "Celebrate Me" attitude that prevails in our country, and it is only magnified in the entertainment industries.

The scary part is that the influence of the media on our young people is stronger than ever before. So the prospect of turning the tide is very daunting.

How did we get on this "Me, Myself and I" path? I believe it actually began in the most unassuming and best-intentioned way.

Where Did We Get Off-track?

I have a hypothesis about when and how we began to lose our national sense of humility. And what's amazing is that it was a subtle 25- to 30-year transition that began with the best of intentions.

By the early 1960s, America had entered a period of self-examination, calling into question a number of elements of the political and social status quo.

- *Are all people created equal?*

- *If so, why are Black people being beaten in the streets of Selma?*

- *How can we make sure that Communism doesn't spread throughout the world?*

- *Is it OK for a woman to want a career?*

All of these were legitimate and morally relevant questions to be asked, especially given the historic value placed upon equality and liberty in the United States. We wanted to make sure we were walking the talk.

From there, however, things took an unexpected turn. In the 1970s the healthy self-examination turned into a more embittered self-criticism.

- *Why are we still in Vietnam?*

- *Why aren't our leaders being more forthcoming about Cambodia, Watergate, Agent Orange, etc.?*

- *Why can't we seem to eradicate poverty in the richest country in the world?*

While these, too, were relevant questions to be asked, I believe they led us toward self-flagellation and a sense of helplessness. We had some pretty significant social challenges facing us as a nation and as individuals. And it was becoming clear that there were no easy solutions to be had.

Remember the forced busing program in Boston in the early '70s? The best-intended policy (school desegregation) still ended up subjecting school kids, their families and most of the city to far more personal discomfort and discord than anyone deserved.

In response to this era of soul-searching, the movement encouraging self-help and self-actualization came into prominence. The rise in popularity of self-proclaimed guru/authors, the increased curiosity in eastern religions, the often fanatical pursuit of EST and other kinds of personal improvement frameworks were all driven by a belief that we as individuals have the ability to improve ourselves.

Though the '70s have been called the "Me Decade," the focus on self-improvement accelerated through the '80s and continues unabated today.

Self-examination. Self-criticism. Self-help. Self-improvement. What's the common denominator? A focus on *SELF*, which, you'll recall, directly opposes the definition of humility we started with.

The truly humble acknowledge that personal *improvement* is an admirable and worthwhile endeavor. When, however, we allow ourselves to get on the road to personal *perfection*, we find it extremely steep, narrow and impossible for mere mortals to negotiate.

Let me make this a bit more personal.

As a Christian, I find tremendous peace in knowing that I am completely unable to improve myself without His guidance, direction and influence. I'm flawed and limited in my abilities, but I love a God who cares for me, wants only the best for me, and can do all things.

I've come to learn that when I am an active and obedient participant in the plans that He has for me, the outcomes are consistently positive. I know that I am most effective—as a husband, as a father, as a leader, as a citizen—when I subscribe to God's intentions, and sub-vert my own motivations and tendencies.

There have been more occasions than I care to admit when I have tried to manage my own life, outside of God's will for me. And I've botched things every time. Massive sums of money have been squandered, painful lessons have been learned, and emotions have been bruised.

Worst of all, *time has been wasted.*

Please hear me carefully, though. I do not believe that we get to completely abdicate our responsibilities and say "Take it away, Almighty One!" Instead, I believe that we are called to be fully engaged in the growth and development process that God has lined up for all of us.

In Paul's letter to the church in Philippi, he writes that we are to *continue to work out [our] salvation with fear and trembling, for it is God who works in [us] … to act according to his good purpose.*[21] What this says to me is that I need to grab a figurative shovel and get to work. I am not going to fully experience God's good purpose for me unless I'm a vested participant in the effort.

What I want to emphasize is that I believe we need to worry less about trying to manage our own paths through life, because we inevitably end up with sub-optimal outcomes. Instead, I believe we need to ask for Divine guidance and direction, not only to determine how to extract the most from our own existence, but also to learn how we can enhance the lives of those around us.

The irony is that once we are released from the unwinnable race to personal perfection, not only do we enjoy peace of mind, but we also can be lifted to greater levels of personal development and satisfaction. How? By focusing on meeting the needs and desires of others!

To that end, few opportunities are more personally satisfying than participating in a community service project of some kind. Building homes with Habitat For Humanity, volunteering at a soup kitchen, even conducting a canned food drive during the holidays are all ways that many of us give back to those less fortunate.

More dramatically, we are consistently willing to make financial contributions to disaster relief efforts around the world, a fact for which Americans don't receive enough credit.

The interesting thing, though, is that for most of us, it's a once- or twice-a-year effort. It's as if we're putting an "X" in the cosmic "Do something good for others" box, and for the rest of the year, we're understandably focused on our jobs, our bills, our kids, our marriages, our favorite football team, etc.

I maintain that we are at our best as individuals and as a culture when we spend at least as much, if not more, time considering the ways in which we can improve the lot of those around us. And this doesn't have to mean jumping on a plane to feed the starving kids in the Sudan. This move toward selflessness can begin at home.

The talented author and teacher Beth Moore has put forward an excellent hypothesis on why American youths seem to be mired in boredom and apathy. The root cause, she maintains, is that we have been so successful at meeting the *needs* of our children, that we've actually overshot the target.

In this country, most parents are meeting most if not all of their children's *wants* too. And because most American kids today don't have a real perspective on what it means to be in need, they don't have an innate understanding of the importance of serving others' needs. And it's really not their fault that they don't.

If everyone with whom our children come in contact has almost everything he needs and wants, then it requires an extra effort on the part of parents to impart to our children the value of serving others.

I echo Ms. Moore's concern about the lack of a service ethic with many of today's youths because if they don't learn it early, it is highly unlikely that they will adopt it as adults. And we may be developing an entire generation of self-oriented Americans without even the inkling that serving others is a source of personal satisfaction and a means by which they can leave a legacy for themselves.

The bottom line is that we have allowed ourselves to be so focused on our own desires for self-made happiness, self-made wealth and celebrating a self-oriented worldview that we rarely consider the even-greater satisfaction that comes from focusing outward.

The reality that I want to expose is that humility and personal satisfaction can go hand in hand. As do humility and personal success. In fact, humility can be the source of strength and effectiveness as a leader at home, at school and in the marketplace.

How Can We Be Humble and Powerful?

I'm sure many of you are still having trouble getting your heads around that notion that we can be humble yet strong.

My guess is that the reason for your confusion is that we have come to narrowly define the characteristics of strength in America.

A strong person gets what she wants. A strong person makes things happen, by any means necessary. A strong person sometimes imposes his will on others to reach his goals. And, more often than not, strong people are seen as successful people.

When we think of strong leaders, they are often larger-than-life, "take no prisoners" types who wield their power with confidence, and project a visible air of what we've come to think of as authority. They are not often endowed with the gene of self-effacement.

We think of people like George Patton. Legendary coach Bobby Knight. These men, at the top of their respective fields, who led (and continue to lead) with a firm hand and who projected a supreme sense of confidence in their abilities and judgment. We've defined humility as the willingness to consider the needs of others before your own. If humility requires being modest, patient, and gentle, then we might be hard-pressed to apply this label to these great and successful men.

When we consider the accomplishments of these men, they would clearly be classified as strong leaders, according to most definitions. I maintain, however, that there are others who have enjoyed equal if not greater success in the same fields of endeavor as Patton and Knight. And these other men would more closely embody the para-dox of exerting strength *through* humility.

General George S. Patton was a highly decorated commander in the US Army in World War II. By any measure, his was an outstanding career, marked by an impressive record of successes over his entire life.

Patton was a man endowed with many gifts, having a keen intellect and superior athletic abilities. He was multi-lingual, a vigorous stu-dent of history, and he competed in the 1912 Olympics as a pen-tathlete.

But it was on the battlefield that Patton enjoyed his greatest glory. The highlight of his career was his remarkable leadership of the Third Army. The official After Action Report summarizes their accomplishments thusly:

In nine months and eight days of campaigning, Third U.S. Army compiled a record of offensive operations that could only be measured in superlatives, for not only did the Army's achievements astonish the world, but its deeds in terms of figures challenged the imagination. [22]

This force of more than 430,000 troops liberated or captured more than 12,000 cities, 27 of which were home to at least 50,000 citizens. Patton not only moved the Third Army farther and faster than any force of its size in American history, but he also displayed masterful tactical skill in the rapid counterattack required to relieve the 101st Airborne during the Battle of the Bulge.[23] George Patton was the consummate warrior and a highly effective leader.

Patton was known to have great affinity for his troops. He often told his men that he was proud to fight alongside them, and he constantly expressed confidence in their ability to successfully complete their missions. And his men typically responded to his leadership.

In the words of Maj. Isaac White:

You might not have loved him, but you respected him and admired him and you wanted to put out for him.... Every unit in the division developed a very fierce and intense pride in its accomplishments. [24]

But Patton's flamboyance and hard-and-fast adherence to his own intuitions could never be construed as humble. His unique personal image—featuring a highly polished helmet, non-traditional riding pants and cavalry boots, and ivory-handled, nickel-plated pistols—were indicative of his desire to stand apart from the norm and call attention to himself. [25]

More damning than his attire, though, was his willingness to flirt with the borders of insubordination in order to satisfy his need for the limelight.

By all accounts, Patton was his own man, and was inclined to pursue his own strategies, even when they conflicted with the orders of his commanding officers. Following his successful turnaround of the II (Second) Corps in Northern Africa, Patton was given command of the Seventh Army as part of the invasion of Sicily. His orders were to liberate the western half of the island, and his rival, British General Bernard Montgomery, was charged with securing the eastern half.

Instead, Patton drove his troops through western Sicily, liberated Palermo and then pressed eastward to Messina, effectively stealing Montgomery's thunder. [26]

We might say that, in wartime, the end justifies the means. It's hard, though, to avoid the reality that Patton's actions, while ultimately successful, were at least partially driven by his unwillingness to share success with his British counterpart. And, by pursuing such an aggressive path across Sicily, he doubtlessly put the lives of his men at risk. There's no way to see any glimpse of humility in Patton's leadership repertoire.

In contrast, General Omar Bradley often modeled humble leadership, and eventually became Patton's superior officer. Known as the "Soldier's General," Bradley took great pains to consider the impact of his decisions and actions on his men. As a result, he not only earned their respect, but he was rewarded with rapid promotion in the Army.

Upon accepting leadership of the 82nd Infantry Division in February, 1942, Bradley insisted that incoming draftees *were welcomed with military bands; when they were marched directly to their cantonments, they found uniforms, equipment, and a hot meal waiting for them. Such practices did much to boost the morale of often-bewildered inductees.* [27]

Bradley understood that the drafted soldiers were entering a new world for which they were likely not prepared. To get the best from them, he knew that bolstering their morale was a critical first step.

Similarly, after assuming command of the II Corps from General Patton in April of 1943, Bradley focused his efforts on convincing his own men and their British counterparts that they were on par with the best units in the war and that the II Corps would never again experience the kind of rout they endured at Kasserine Pass in February of that same year. [28]

Bradley's ability to cast a compelling vision for his troops was admirable. He embodied the maxim that leadership expert John Maxwell coined years later: *People don't care how much you see until they see how much you care.*[29]

Bradley knew that to succeed he needed his men to gain confidence in him and his ability to lead them to victory, but he did that by helping the men believe in themselves.

By V-E Day, Bradley's 12th Army Group was the largest ever commanded by an American general. It consisted of The First, Third, Ninth and Fifteenth Armies, a force comprising 12 corps, 48 divisions, and 1.3 million men. He consistently impressed his superior officers with his calm and effective presence in times of crisis, and with his effective leadership of even the most challenging subordinates, including Patton.

Perhaps this quote summarizes the impact that these two great leaders had on one another:

It is difficult, for example, to imagine Patton without Bradley, who exploited the talents of that volatile commander as well as any man could have done. [30]

The role of head coach in the realm of athletics is the nearest analogue to the general officer on the battlefield. Though the stakes riding on victory and loss in combat make the outcome of a ballgame completely insignificant, the impact of effective leadership on the playing field is still undeniable.

The head coach—especially at a major American university—is responsible for the successful recruitment of talented players and the development and implementation of a philosophy and system that fits his team's abilities. This system needs to be implemented by his staff and, ultimately, winning seasons are expected to be produced.

When basketball fans refer to "The General," they are speaking (respectfully) of Coach Bobby Knight. Winner of three college basketball national championships and a four-time National Coach of the Year, Coach Knight has enjoyed success at West Point, Indiana University and Texas Tech University.

Coach Knight's success lies not only in his extensive knowledge of the game, but also in his drive for perfection. His national championship team of 1976 finished the season with a 32–0 record, and remains the last team to have a perfect record. One of his star players, Quinn Buckner, said of Knight, *I think he's constantly searching ... for the perfect game and he honestly believes it's out there. That's what moves him.*[31]

Knight's leadership rises and falls on his firm insistence on individual and team discipline. Known for his outbursts and tirades on the sidelines of his games (this is the man who threw a chair onto the playing floor *during* a game), few things set Knight off more than a lapse in concentration or departure from the disciplined game plan he has devised. In fact, Knight has admitted that he is prone to angry outbursts. *Yes, of course I do have a temper, but many times what peo-*

ple read as anger was my being extremely passionate toward helping kids become the best they can be at whatever they're going to do. [32]

Coach Knight's demanding style was exerted on all players, regardless of their talent or status on the team. He made clear that he would have no qualms about benching even his most talented athletes if he believed he was not seeing their best effort. His simple explanation: *That's the way we handle ego at Indiana.* [33]

Another of Knight's star players, Steve Alford, described the paradox that Knight's demanding style presents:

I knew I was in the hands of a truly great basketball coach. I was less certain, however, of what kind of person he was. I couldn't understand the need to intimidate people. Everybody around him—players, assistant coaches, faculty, sportswriters—seemed uncomfortable in his presence. [34]

Intimidation is a common lever of authority and leadership. It is not, however, consistent with the concept of humble leadership. The autocratic, fear-based model of direction is certainly effective, to a point. Given Coach Knight's 800+ victories, his success at the highest levels of college basketball is undeniable.

But one must wonder if Knight's teams could have broken through to even more national championships over the four decades of his coaching career. Did Knight's style perhaps cap his success?

If national championships are the ultimate indicator of college basketball coaching success, then Coach John Wooden's tally of 10
titles makes him the undisputed king.

Known for his quietly intense and cerebral coaching style, "The
Wizard of Westwood" led UCLA to those ten championships in the
course of an incredible twelve-year period. He, like Knight, enjoyed
undefeated seasons—four of them. His teams often featured outstanding individual talents such as Lewis Alcindor (now Kareem
Abdul-Jabbar) and Bill Walton. But more often, Wooden's teams
were characterized by selfless play and a collective willingness by
each player to fill the role required by Wooden's system.

Coach Wooden thought of himself first as a teacher. He simply
enjoyed *watching youngsters improve. If I didn't see improvement in
my youngsters from the beginning of the year to the end, I thought, I'm
to blame, because I'm the teacher. When I had players that didn't
improve to the degree I thought they should, I felt responsible and it
bothered me.*[35]

In the same sense that Coach Knight sought to extract the best performance possible from his players, Coach Wooden set his sights on
drawing improved performance from his team over the course of a
season.

In contrast to Knight's bullying leadership style, however, Coach
Wooden would prefer to "model" the kind of control and compo-
sure that he expected from his players.

My feeling was that I tried to teach players that if they lose their temper or get out of control, they will get beat.[36]

On another occasion, Coach Wooden put it more directly:

I tried to conduct myself in such a way that I wanted my players to act. I think our youngsters, whether they be basketball players or our children at home, need models more than they need critics.[37]

Wooden's coaching philosophy is summarized in his "Pyramid of Success." The Pyramid features fifteen personal attributes that Coach Wooden believes were instrumental for success in sports and in life. As an example, one building block in the pyramid is "Team Spirit." In his own words, Coach Wooden describes the importance of Team Spirit this way:

We all want to do well and receive individual praise. That's fine if the praise comes because your 'individual' effort was something that contributed to the improvement or strength of the group, the team, whatever your team is: sports, business, family, or community. Praise that comes because of your contribution to the group is the kind of praise I prize.

Team Spirit means you are willing to sacrifice personal considerations for the welfare of all. That defines a team player.[38]

Clearly, Wooden's desire for team spirit reflects his appreciation for humility from his players. But Wooden also believes that those in positions of leadership need to fully understand the nature of their relationship with team members.

I think anyone in a position of supervision, if they're not listening to those under them, they're not going to get good results. The supervisor must make sure that all of those under his supervision understand they're working with him, not for him. [39]

Coach Wooden's coaching/teaching style displays an appreciation that, to extract the best from a team, the leader needs to somehow tap the team members' willingness to submit to the overall goals of the team. To do so requires the leader to display a humble willingness to do the same.

The exceptional leaders show themselves willing to set aside the standard levers of influence like position and intimidation. This is a key trait of humble leadership, one that Coach Wooden displayed masterfully over his storied career. Yet it clearly did not come at the expense of his strength or effectiveness as a leader.

21st-century Humility

I don't want anyone to come away with the impression that humility is completely dead in today's world. While the examples we have just explored are drawn from the last century, be assured that there remain outstanding examples of humble yet influential, relevant, and highly successful individuals.

These are Americans who have publicly and notably demonstrated a sensitivity to their calling, and have opted to redirect attention from their own personal successes, instead using that notoriety to enhance the lives of others.

The 2006 Winter Olympic Games in Turin provided a platform for an interesting set of American archetypes.

You had the "American Hotdog," best illustrated by Lindsay Jacobellis, the snowboard racer who lost the gold medal within yards of the finish by trying an unnecessary trick as part of a premature celebration.

(I actually give Lindsay a lot of credit, though, for staying true to the snowboard ethos that starts and ends with having fun. And she's displayed a lot of perspective, class and poise by pointing out that she did win a medal, enjoyed her experience, and that the Olympics are still just *games*.)

Then we had the "Whining American," a role played to pitch perfection by Johnny Weir. When asked about his poor performance, he blamed the fact that he missed his bus to the arena, which threw him off his game and left him spiritually bereft. "I didn't feel my aura," he said. "I was black inside."[40]

C'mon, if you're a world class athlete (yes, I think skaters are athletes), then I expect that your psyche is resilient enough to endure some bumps in the road. It wasn't like someone took a pipe to his knee during his warm-up....

Of course, there was Bode Miller, the much-hyped skier who was probably the biggest American disappointment at those Games. While some folks have held up Bode as the poster boy for the "Ugly American," I think his behavior more accurately put him in the role of the "Apathetic American."

Here was a guy who was a strong candidate to win as many as five medals, and he did nothing to dispel those expectations. Ever the iconoclast, he said before the Games that "I kind of take pride in the fact that I do things my own way." [41]

What Bode called doing things his own way looked to the rest us like a spectacular failure to perform.

Mental errors, inadequate preparation, and too much partying all probably contributed to the poor showing. But Miller lost tons of respect when he adopted an unfathomable insouciance, a shoulder-shrugging, "whatever, man" attitude about his losses.

All of a sudden, he seemed to be asking what the fuss was about, insisting that he really didn't see the big deal about not even coming within sniffing distance of a medal.

Apathy is often a salve for an unwillingness to admit failure, but that doesn't make it any more attractive to see.

Miller could have shown himself to be graceful in defeat, a stand-up guy who said, "Sorry, but I just couldn't get into my groove this week. I wish I'd done better, and I know there are a lot of disappointed folks out there. No one is more upset than I am ..." Instead we got this gem:

"It's been an awesome two weeks. I got to party and socialize at an Olympic level."

Heckuva job, Bode.

Americans are often thought to be more comfortable as individuals than as members of a team, and there is probably some merit to this stereotype. However, when American athletes are invited to be part of a team, one would hope that the team spirit would overcome this genetic predisposition to make it "all about me."

Instead, we were treated to the public bickering between Shani Davis and Chad Hedrick. Nothing is as unbecoming as the public airing of dirty laundry, and these two talented speedskaters saw fit to feud with one another in full view of the world media. It was the "Selfish American," in stereo!

Regardless of the basis of their disagreement (it was basically a difference of opinion over whether individuals competing in an individual sport should feel obligated to participate in a team relay event), there was no reason for this dispute to ever leave the locker room. It negated the positives of their excellent performances in Torino.

As an added bonus, we got to see an African-American man and a White American man acting like anything but teammates. So much for "Ebony and Ivory" in the USA.

So in the midst of this sea of negative, unseemly, embarrassing athletes doing nothing to acquit themselves favorably on the world stage, we saw a glimmer of hope. His name is Joey Cheek, and his performance as a champion was exceeded only by his generosity and humility.

After winning the 500M speed-skating event, Cheek decided to use his moment in the spotlight to do something other than mouth "Hi Mom!" at the camera or give a shout out to his bros back home.

Instead, he made a singular statement about our need to maintain perspective when we celebrate successes in the world of sports. He also showed himself willing to redirect the attention and rewards he was getting for his athletic prowess, and apply them to a cause that needs all the help it can get.

In Cheek's own words:

I have always felt if I ever do something big like this I want to be able to give something back.

I love what I do, it's great fun, but honestly, it's a pretty ridiculous thing: I skate around in tights. If you keep it in perspective, I've trained my whole life for this but it's not that big a deal.

But because I skated well I have a few seconds of microphone time. And I know how news cycles work. Tomorrow there will be another gold medalist. So I can either gush how wonderful I feel or use it for something.

So I am donating the entire [winning] sum the USOC gives me [$25,000] to an organization, 'Right to Play,' that Johan Olav Kos [the

Norwegian icon who won three gold medals in 1994 in Lillehammer]
either started or gave to in 1994. It helps refugees in Chad, where there
are over 60,000 persons displaced from their homes. I am going to be
asking all of the Olympic sponsors if they will match my donation.

In Sudan, there have been tens of thousands of people killed. My govern-
ment has labeled it genocide. Hopefully, if we can stabilize the region,
with U.N. or U.S. pressure, we can go in and start programs for refugees
there.

Johan has lived his life in a manner I hope to live my life. I can only
hope to fit in his large shoes.[42]

Wow.

At the moment that he sat at the pinnacle of his sport, after years of
work and sacrifice, this young man exploded all expectations. He
had the presence of mind, the poise, the media savvy, and simply
the willingness to reach out to Sudanese refugees who were thinking
about almost anything but some American speedskater.

Cheek was hailed as a breath of fresh air, and he is a reminder that
The Generous American is another exemplar we have cultivated
over the years. But for me, it was his orientation toward others, his
desire to pour himself and his resources into the lives of the downtrodden without any desire for the accolades he received that most
impressed me. I pray that millions of other young citizens saw and
were likewise touched by Joey Cheek's actions.

That's the way American humility will continue to survive: by modeling it for the young so that they can see that personal success and humility needn't be oxymoronic.

I do hope we see more Joey Cheeks and fewer Bode Millers, not just in the next Olympic Games, but simply walking around our school campuses in the future. If we don't, then we should be prepared to be criticized for losing one of the elements of our character that was most admired by our fellow citizens of the world.

Humility and Pride

It's been said that pride is the opposite of humility, and that the two cannot co-exist.

Hold on. What's wrong with pride? Can't I be proud of my kids? Proud of my workmanship? Proud to be an American?

We are a proud people, we deeply value our national pride, and we celebrate it whenever we can. Why shouldn't we? It helps to draw us together as a people. Our pride in our way of life is our rallying cry.

I believe that there are two related pitfalls that await us when we're trying to balance humility and pride.

First, let's agree upon a definition of pride. The most innocuous is "A sense of one's own proper dignity or value; self-respect." Another one that is relatively harmless is "Pleasure or satisfaction taken in an achievement, possession, or association." [43]

While neither of these would seem to be inappropriate attitudes, both still hold the risk of engendering self-orientation. As we've seen, a focus on ourselves tends to be a slippery slope that has the potential to morph into self-centeredness.

The most extreme form of pride is what the Greeks originally referred to as *hubris*. This is the over-the-top belief in our own abilities, which often leads to the assumption that we are immune to failure. In many cultures' folklore, there are myths and legends where a character afflicted with this attitude is destined to enjoy a dramatic tumble from grace.

The proverb "pride goes before a fall" speaks to this notion that anyone who gets too much of "the big head" is bound to be taken down a notch. And most of us would agree that this form of pride is frankly offensive and not something that we, as Americans, would care to cultivate.

There is, however, a more innocuous form of pride that also needs to be leavened with humility.

When we celebrate successes, either individually or as a people, we need to take care to acknowledge how much of that success was facilitated by our circumstances versus our own efforts. Even celebrating the achievements of others (like our children) opens the door to the sense that what was achieved or obtained resulted exclusively from the work of the individual.

Let me explain.

It requires a great deal of introspection and a lot of practice to look at our accomplishments and readily acknowledge all of the inputs and influences that fed into that success. Most of us don't consider how the mere fact that we live in a country with amazing resources facilitates even run-of-the-mill "wins."

For example, my daughter is a talented young pianist and every time she plays at a recital, I am filled with pride and joy. She has always been a focused young lady, and playing the piano allows her to immerse herself in the pieces she plays.

As a result, she enjoys her preparation, she enjoys performing, and she enjoys the audience feedback. We proudly celebrate her dedication and her accomplishments all the time.

My son started playing soccer this season, and you would have thought the kid had a soccer ball in his crib. (His dad's own soccer career ended in the Carter administration, so his is all God-given talent.)

When other parents would come up to us after a game and compliment him on his play, you can be sure that my chest would swell, and I would thank them for the kind words. There's no prouder feeling that having my kids succeed.

Here's where we often lose perspective.

Sure, a lot of time, effort and talent plays into our kids' successes. But I have to acknowledge that if we didn't live in a country of plenty, a secure country of opportunity, there's no guarantee that any of these accomplishments would come to fruition.

If I had to stand guard at my home to keep guerilla fighters from taking my daughter to war, I don't think piano lessons would be in the picture.

If we were eating one meal a week, I don't think my son would have the boundless energy on the soccer field that he does.

If we were living a hand-to-mouth, disease-plagued, drought-stricken existence, we wouldn't celebrate these kinds of leisure activities. We would celebrate another day's survival.

This is not to say that we should feel guilty for the bounty we enjoy. My point is simply that we need to temper the pride in our (or our loved ones') accomplishments with the realization that we have all been blessed to live, work and play from a position of privilege.

We demonstrate humility when we appreciate that, and we moderate our celebrations accordingly.

How Do We Bring Back Humility?

While I'm reluctant to offer a prescription for humility, I do believe there are at least nine steps any of us can take to begin to reverse the tide of self-orientation that has been accelerating in this country over the last fifty years.

As you review the list and consider the merits of the suggestions, try to think of them in the context of your everyday life. None of these require wholesale changes to your beliefs or social customs.

But it is my belief that these efforts will, indeed, help us turn our mental and spiritual focus outward, allowing us to recall the merits of humility and the fruits borne from a selfless attitude.

1. Realize it's not always about you

File this under "Blindingly Obvious Insights." As we determined at the outset, the desire to consider the interests of others is fundamental to a humble attitude.

But try this exercise: in the course of a single day, count the number of times you do something strictly to meet your own needs, desires, or interests.

How often do you say, or even think, "I," "my," or "mine"? How do you determine where you go for lunch? What motivates you to switch lanes in traffic? At the end of the day, how do you decide how you are going to spend your time? What television shows are watched in your home? Why?

There are probably dozens of very small decisions that are made "because I wanted to …", "because I felt like it …", or "because that would enable me to…." Not to worry, though. We know that our own self-interests are somewhat hardwired into us.

However, we have a tremendous capacity to subvert our own desires and to impact the lives of those around us. The trouble is that we don't always do so.

Put plainly, we often feel entitled to fulfill our own wishes, and that sense of entitlement can often deaden our sensitivities to the needs of others.

It is unreasonable to expect that we will make a full reversal and become completely selfless. But we should challenge ourselves to take note of how much we do for our own satisfaction, and where we might find a moment to consider "you," "yours," or even "us."

2. Change your success scorecard

Today, we tend to think in "zero sum" terms. If someone wins, then someone else must lose. For this reason, any time we are not maximizing our own returns/winnings/benefits/satisfaction, then we think that we are not as successful as we might otherwise be.

The remedy to this is easy: Just change our definition of success.

How? First, by acknowledging that the zero sum perspective is, at best, selfish, and at worst dysfunctional in a society where collaboration and cooperation are requirements for civil co-existence.

If every winner produces a loser, then, at any point in time, at least 50% of the world is unhappy, dissatisfied, and likely plotting ways to get back into the winner's circle on his next engagement.

Talk about a waste of time and energy.

Instead, determine your success, at least in part, by how often you are contributing to someone else's well-being.

What if you measured your own level of fulfillment by watching the reaction someone else has when you provide an unsolicited or unexpected service?

You might be surprised that when you focus your energies outward, and strive to derive pleasure from deferring to others in a variety of situations, you will almost certainly begin to appreciate the sense of purpose that results.

The point is that once we choose to measure success in a more self-less manner, we have a greater chance of actually achieving real, sustainable personal satisfaction. Best of all, the zero-sum world begins to be truly win-win.

3. Take inventory of your talents, and put them to work for others

All of us are endowed with natural strengths and talents. (A great book to help clarify yours is *Now, Discover Your Strengths* by Marcus Buckingham and Donald Clifton.)

Once we understand what these talents are, we should seek out situations to put them to use, as often as possible, for the benefit of others.

You might say, "Well, I have a job, and I get a paycheck for doing that job. That allows me to put food on my table for my family. Mission accomplished."

There's no denying that we need to make sure we're tending to our personal needs and obligations, and that is one of the primary ways we leverage at least some of our talents.

But I would challenge you to look at a more extensive inventory of your gifts. Be sure to include those that may not have any commercial value but do have the potential to benefit others. (Remember, that's part of your new definition of success.)

Think about the things that you genuinely enjoy doing, be they actual hobbies, or just ways you enjoy spending time. Then find some way to devote a small portion of each week exploring how that particular talent can be used to help someone else.

If you enjoy puttering around the house fixing and tweaking things, then volunteer to help elderly citizens with odd fix-it jobs around their houses.

If you have a gift for hospitality, but don't necessarily want to invite a bunch of people to your home, why not offer to help the volunteers at a homeless shelter make their facility just a little bit more inviting to their guests?

Ideally, you'll be refreshed and energized by flexing "talent muscles" that you don't often get to exercise and, best of all, you'll be serving others in the process.

4. Listen to silence

How often do you enjoy total silence?

First of all, *finding* total silence is not an easy task in today's tech-laden times. There's seemingly always a hum of an air-conditioner fan, the white noise of a PC, or more obvious mechanical noises emanating from the streets around our homes and workplaces.

No mater how hard it is, however, I strongly encourage you to find a way to get somewhere that you can actually hear your own heart beating.

This might require a trip to the countryside, though even there you might be challenged by sounds of nature. Or, I'm told that noise-canceling headphones can come close to achieving total silence … as long as they aren't plugged into an MP3 player.

Why is finding silence so important?

You might be surprised to learn that it is not to get in touch with your inner self or to focus your thinking.

I believe that when we are alone and "quiet our hearts," we actually realize how relatively insignificant our day-to-day concerns are. Before we find silence, it seems like we are always worried about something that needs to be done, said, tended to, or fixed.

But if we make the effort on a regular basis to be still and listen to silence, we gain perspective and we are energized. We realize that our personal concerns are often less daunting than they originally seemed.

Sometimes, we find that our creativity is sparked by eliminating the noise from our lives (literally and figuratively). We often discover breakthrough solutions simply because we can apply more of our intellectual bandwidth to the dilemmas we're facing.

Most importantly, though, I believe that by aggressively seeking quiet time, it actually frees up some of our mental and emotional capacity, much of which can then be used to serve others.

Personally, my quiet time each morning is invaluable, and it starts my day off right. I pray, read, and sometimes just let my mind wander.

And it has amazed me how quickly my thoughts get to the point where I'm saying to myself "Enough about me. What about Carmen (my wife)? Are the kids getting the teaching and influence we want them to have? And what about the team at work? How can I help everyone on the team be even a little bit better?"

Now, it's one thing to think about serving others and humbling ourselves enough to think of their needs. It's something completely different to act upon those ideas and intentions.

Still, by first finding a way to slow down and bring clarity to our thoughts, we can at least begin the process of humbling ourselves. And, given the pace and the rampant distractions foisted upon us by our world today, I believe this is the best way to start.

5. Be anonymously generous

Generosity is an admirable trait. It's hard to find fault with someone who shares her good fortune with others, especially if the giving requires some degree of sacrifice.

Unfortunately, our self-orientation sometimes creeps into our impulses to be generous. We occasionally think about how good it will make us feel to do something generous for someone else. Or we consider, for example, the tax deductibility of a financial donation to a charity.

Let's be clear: This doesn't in any way lessen the positive impact of the gift. This attitude does, however, edify the donor and his contribution more than it should.

Instead, I believe that we should actively seek out opportunities to bless others with unexpected and uncredited generosity.

I don't advocate the clichéd "random acts of kindness," though. I would prefer to see more of us target our acts of kindness and make them extremely relevant and valuable for the recipient. The difference is that the "donors" would go to great lengths to protect their own identity.

As a result, the gift is somehow pristine, more innocent, and unsullied by mixed motives.

More importantly, the giver can be more certain that his intentions were truly selfless in origin.

Why go to all this trouble? Because a fundamental tenet for those with a humble world view is that we should want to do for others and elevate them, regardless of the impact on our own station.

Plus, it would put so much more goodwill into circulation if we simply made a habit of giving with nothing to gain. Even if humility doesn't result, social kindness would certainly enjoy a renaissance.

6. Learn from "Level 5" leaders

In his outstanding study of corporate leadership, *Good to Great*, Jim Collins conducts an exhaustive analysis of several companies that outperformed peer companies in their respective industries over an extended period.

Among the more unexpected success factors to which Collins points is that all of the great companies were led by "Level 5" leaders, who are described as being "a study in duality: modest and willful, humble and fearless."[44]

The thing that we can all learn from these Level 5 leaders is that competence and effective leadership do not have to come at the expense of humility. Rather, one could argue that the healthy focus on the needs of others—employees, customers, voters, parishioners—and the staunch reluctance to believe one's own press is actually integral to a strong leader's portfolio.

If such leaders are pleased but never satisfied with their own performance, and are constantly in search of opportunities to improve the quality and skill of their team members and their organizations, then there is little time left for self-congratulation or potentially distracting victory laps.

At the same time, Collins points out that these humble leaders are by no means weak. The best-known example of this kind of "humble strength," in fact, was President Lincoln. Though he had a modest, self-deprecating personal affect, he was resolute in his convictions, and was willing to endure significant sacrifice—including his own life—to ensure that the Union remained intact. [45]

None of the Level 5 leaders of Collins' great companies were the "Celebrity CEOs" that we have come to celebrate in the last 20 years. Instead, theirs were relatively low-key personalities that masked a firm sense of purpose and resolve to do what was necessary to drive their companies to succeed.

The good news is that, while they may not be leading Fortune 500 companies, there are several examples of Level 5 leaders all around us. They may be school principals, factory supervisors, nurses in intensive care units, construction foremen or church pastors.

You can tell who they are because you'll observe that their organizations are well run and that their team members are engaged. But you won't necessarily see the Level 5 leader demanding center stage with a spotlight. Instead, she is just as likely to point to key members of her core team who "make it all happen."

These individuals have come to realize (either from trial and error, strong mentorship or good home training) that with humility comes a teachability that, in turn, makes a leader incredibly effective at understanding the needs and challenges confronting his team.

We would be wise to strive for this openness and receptivity in an effort to strike Collins' balance of modesty, humility and fearlessness.

7. Serve your way out of difficult times

The uncertainty of life ensures that we will endure our share of personal challenges. No matter if they are physical or financial hardships, family or professional crises, we have a number of ways that we can cope with them. Often, the most effective and comforting means of recovery involves seeking the support of loved ones, allowing for the passage of time, or simply grinning and bearing it.

Unfortunately, many of us tend to spend a fair bit of time stewing in our misery. We wallow in it, wondering what we've done to deserve this spell of misfortune. If we're blessed to have friends and family around, we may lean on them for support and encouragement. But even our family can come to feel burdened by an extended season of someone else's troubles.

Please understand: I know firsthand that we must mourn our losses. I firmly disagree with the concept of hiding our feelings, pretending that the pain isn't present, or believing that we just need to "tough it out." Healing takes time and it is an active process that should not be minimized.

My proposal, however, is that we can accelerate our healing by turning our attentions away from our own troubles, and helping to relieve the burdens of others.

While this isn't always the case, there is a strong likelihood that others in your sphere of influence are experiencing even more pain and challenges than you are. You may not be in a position to do anything other than offer moral support and comfort for those individuals.

But we can create a mutually beneficial arrangement by reaching out to those in need while we are in need. Most people are familiar with the Biblical story of how Jesus fed 5,000 followers with two fish and five loaves of bread. [46]

What's all the more amazing about that story is that, shortly before performing this miracle of compassion and service, Jesus had been informed that his cousin, John the Baptist, had been murdered.

Back in verse 13, we're told Jesus went away to be alone, presumably to mourn. But *the crowds followed him,*[47] and we're told that Jesus had compassion on them and began healing the sick. Not much time could have passed before Jesus turned his attention away from his own sorrow and began tending to the needs of others.

So, while we may not be able to perform supernatural miracles, we absolutely can perform everyday acts of service. And, when we are in the throes of life's challenges, we can help speed our own recovery by pouring our energies into the lives of other people in the midst of their hardships.

Humbling ourselves by serving others leaves everyone involved in a better place.

8. *Take one for the team*

Most of us live, play or work as part of a group. In our homes, on our job sites, in our temples and churches, we are individuals coming together as members of a group, a unit, a team.

As with any team, the success of the group is dependent on the alignment of all interests and objectives, and, in most cases, a great deal of compromise and collaboration.

According to Coach Wooden's Pyramid of Success, team spirit is defined as "an eagerness to sacrifice personal interest or glory for the welfare of all."[48] Simply being a part of a team requires the occasional submission of some of our own interests and desires for the sake of the team.

As the saying goes, there's no "I" in "team" (though some smart aleck soon pointed out that there are an "M" and an "E" ...).

My recommendation is to take this idea of team spirit to a deeper level. The next time there's a task or initiative that promises to be more of a hassle than a source of pleasure or recognition, step up and ask to take responsibility for it. When you do this a few things will happen, all of which will serve to help recalibrate your humility antennae.

First, you will probably be the recipient of a fair bit of gratitude from other members of the organization who will consider that they've dodged a bullet.

You, though, will be seen as a person of unique character and self-lessness. You'll hear things like "there's a stand-up guy," "what a mensch," and "better him than me."

But you won't have done this simply to get high-fives from your team members.

The real win for you will be the realization that there is personal satisfaction in leaving one's ego aside and doing something for others that makes the team better. The fact that your teammates are grateful is just the start. The important realization is that you will have done something to make the team better. And as a member of that team your investment has gone up a bit because of the kind of sacrifices you've made.

As I mentioned earlier, I don't particularly care for check-the-box generosity. But if there's a manifold blessing that can be enjoyed—by the beneficiary of the actions, by the person showing the generosity, by the society at large—then we're talking about a more intentional brand of largesse.

And that is the foundation of humility.

9. Submit to real authority

The highly regarded "12 Step" programs that have helped millions learn to manage their addictions feature an intriguing statement about the role of humility in their recovery.

Fully 6 of the 12 steps include either an overt reference to God or to a *Power greater than ourselves [that] could restore us to sanity.*[49]

In fact, Step 7 requires that recovering addicts have *humbly asked God to remove [their] shortcomings.* [50]

This is instructive for all of us, even if we do not suffer from the pain and destruction of addictions. The truth is that all of us would do well to acknowledge that, left to our own devices, there is only so much we can do for ourselves in this world.

Despite the fact that most Americans are encouraged from childhood to be independent and to try to control their own destiny, the reality is that "destiny management" is not something we should leave to amateurs … like us.

And if we're honest with ourselves, many of us secretly want to turn over accountability for our lives to someone—or something—else.

The reason for this desire to give the reins of our lives to an outside agent is perfectly logical: once we've had a taste of the uncertainty, the challenges, the risks and the weight of making our own way on earth, most of us come to the realization that we're just not up to the task.

In my opinion, this is a very healthy admission which inherently takes our focus off of ourselves. Once we cede control of our lives and our happiness to our God, then we are free from the burden of self-actualization and self-improvement and self-orientation.

We are, instead, willing to subvert our own needs, wants, and desires in order to serve others. We don't need to worry about the zero-sum equation because we've gotten out of that game and are measuring personal fulfillment with a new scorecard.

The sad part is that, while many Americans profess a belief in God, or at least to be "spiritual" people, too many of us seek truth from belief systems that espouse a focus on achieving maximum personal fulfillment.

We've already established that seeking purpose by turning inward is rarely a recipe for success. What's so important about the references to God in the 12 Steps is that they hammer home the point that we are simply not capable of properly directing our lives.

And one does not have to be an addict to appreciate this.

Here's the unavoidable logic: if we believe that God exists, and we believe Him to be all powerful, the Creator of the universe, why would we want to seize authority over our lives from Him?

If He is all-knowing, why would we try to second-guess His directions?

Why do we have trouble obeying His commands, even if we don't always understand His intentions?

For most of us, the answer to these fundamental questions is that we are reluctant to submit to authority. In fact, if we think "humility" is a tough concept for modern Americans to get our heads around, try telling someone to "submit" to someone else.

"You lost me at hello…."

As it happens, though, humility and submission go hand in hand. And because most of us, frankly, have gotten out of the practice of showing any deference to one another, one good way to relearn the process is by submitting to real, all-powerful Divine authority.

Because once we admit to our earthly shortcomings, then pride, ego and attitude get balanced by a greater sense of perspective.

And once we begin to acknowledge our relative impotence, we are able to engage with one another from a place of humility.

What About Carrying the Big Stick?

A number of people have asked me if I intended this book to be an evangelism tool.

The short answer is no.

I've made a number of references to my own faith, and how humility is rooted in an acknowledgement that as much as we might think of ourselves, we are still subject to a Higher Authority.

Please understand: I would love it if this book caused readers to re-examine their own spirituality and draw closer to God.

Candidly, however, I just don't think most people are ready for that step yet.

I don't think most people are ready to acknowledge how much of our personal drama is rooted in a disproportionate concern for our own interests.

I can't see someone embracing a deeper faith in Christ without understanding how we need to reduce our inflated faith in ourselves.

My goal with this book was simply to begin chipping away at the self-orientation we all struggle with, and begin encouraging a self-lessness that makes us better and stronger as individuals and as a people.

So maybe this is really a "prevangelism" tool.

The great irony is that the "big stick" of influence that we all seek is also empowered by the humility found in "speaking softly."

Think about how many people of influence—political, economic, religious, social—have cultivated humility and selflessness as personal attributes and as levers to advance their causes.

Lincoln. Humble … and one of the greatest American presidents.

Gandhi. Humble … and helped end colonialism and achieve Indian independence.

Mother Teresa. Humble … and focused the attention of the world on the abject poverty in Calcutta.

The Dalai Lama. Humble … and fighting for the cause of Tibetan sovereignty in a most dignified fashion.

Dr. King. Humble … and helped Americans acknowledge and begin to reverse their traditions of inequality.

What is encouraging is that these are just some of the best-known humble leaders. There are so many others whom you and I will never meet who will continue to exercise their leadership with a "team first" attitude.

My hope and prayer is that this book helps add to those ranks: the relatively unknown, almost certainly unheralded citizens who look at themselves and realize that a change is in order.

They appreciate that much of what they have come to embrace as American ideals is rooted in fundamentals like humility, integrity, and service.

I will be so excited if and when humility ceases to be an anachronism, but instead becomes a new counter-cultural worldview.

If young Americans especially began to realize that the "check me out!" attitude is so last century, we will be heading in the right direction.

When they look at their prospective role models and embrace peers like Joey Cheek as someone who walks the talk, we will begin building momentum for humility.

Once young influencers begin to speak out and take action on behalf of others—in this country and around the world—the seeds of humility will be planted in good soil.

When they help the rest of us appreciate that because much has been given to Americans, much will be required, we will most certainly see a renaissance of American Humility.

We will again be speaking softly and carrying the big stick of influence and authenticity and credibility.

And we will go far.

Endnotes

Note: Due to the dynamic nature of the World Wide Web, some URLs referenced below may have changed or now require a fee to download it from an online archive.

We will work to secure the rights to reprint those articles on our own website. Please visit www.speaksoftly.com to monitor our progress.

1. John 13:3–5, *The Holy Bible, New International Version (NIV)* International Bible Society, Zondervan, Grand Rapids, 1984.

2. Bush, George W., *Presidential Debate, October 12, 2000,* Online NewsHour, NewsHour with Jim Lehrer transcript, http://www.pbs.org/newshour/bb/politics/july-dec00/for-policy_10–12.html.

3. Roosevelt, Theodore, *Quotations of Theodore Roosevelt,* The Theodore Roosevelt Association, http://www.theodore roosevelt.org/life/quotes.htm.

4. Temple, William, *WorldofQuotes.com,* http://www.worldof quotes.com/topic/Gifts/1/index.html.

5. Washington, George, *Washington's "Earnest Prayer,"* Historic Valley Forge, http://www.ushistory.org/valleyforge/washing ton/earnestprayer.html.

6. Ibid.

7. Adams, John, *Thoughts on Government*, April 1776 Papers 4:86–93, http://www.constitution.org/jadams/thoughts.htm .

8. Adams, John, from a letter to his granddaughter Caroline, http://www.coxontool.com/index.php/Clippings/WalkHumbly .

9. Adams, John, from a diary entry on February 22, 1756, http://www.worldviewweekend.com/secure/institute/book/chapters/arpoagg.html .

10. Jefferson, Thomas, *Ethical Egoism*, Wikipedia, http://en.wikipedia.org/wiki/Ethical_egoism .

11. Jefferson, Thomas, *Thomas Jefferson,* Wikiquote, http://en.wikiquote.org/wiki/Thomas_Jefferson.

12. Isaacson, Walter, *Citizen Ben's Great Virtues*, Time Online Edition, The Amazing Adventures of Ben Franklin, July 7, 2003, Vol. 162 No. 1, http://www.time.com/time/2003/franklin/bffranklin4.html.

13. Ibid

14. Ibid

15. Lincoln, Abraham, *Proclamation of a Day of Fasting by the President of the United States of America*, The History Place, http://www.historyplace.com/lincoln/proc-3.htm.

16. Ibid.

17. Ibid.

18. Ibid

19. Lincoln, Abraham, *Proclamation Appointing a National Fast Day*, Abraham Lincoln: Christian, http://www.eadshome. com/Lincoln.htm .

20. Marshall, George C., *Remarks of Secretary of State George C. Marshall at the Harvard University Commencement Exercises, June 5, 1947*, The Marshall plan—Investment in Peace: Marshall Speech, http://usinfo.state.gov/usa/infousa/facts/mar shall/pam-sp.htm .

21. Philippians 2:12, *New International Version (NIV)* International Bible Society, Zondervan, Grand Rapids, 1984.

22. Axelrod, Alan, *Patton on Leadership*, Prentice Hall Press, Paramus, N.J., 1999, 9.

23. Ibid.

24. Ibid.

25. Wikipedia.org, *George S. Patton*, http://en.wikipedia.org/ wiki/George S. Patton.

26. Ibid.

27. Kirkpatrick, Dr. Charles E., *Omar Nelson Bradley*, CMH Online, http://www.army.mil/cmh-pg/brochures/bradley/ bradley.htm.

28. Ibid.

29. Maxwell, John C., *Developing the Leader Within You*, Thomas Nelson Publishers, Nashville, 1993, 154.

30. Kirkpatrick, Dr. Charles E., *Omar Nelson Bradley*, CMH Online, http://www.army.mil/cmh-pg/brochures/bradley/ bradley.htm.

31. Snook, Scott A.; Perlow, Leslie A.; and DeLacey, Brian J., *Coach Knight: The Will to Win*, Harvard Business School, Boston, 2005.

32. Knight, Bob, with Bob Hammel, *Knight: My Story*, Thomas Dunne Books, New York, 2002, 374.

33. Knight, Bob, *Favorite Coach Knight Quotes*, EZboard.com, http://p200.ezboard.com/faseasononthebrinkfrm2.showMessage?topicID=7.topic .

34. Alford, Steve, with John Garrity, *Playing For Knight: My Six Seasons with Coach Knight*, Simon & Schuster, New York, 1990, 33–34.

35. ESPN.com, *10 Burning Questions for John Wooden*, http://espn.go.com/page2/s/questions.wooden.html.

36. Rubel, Shelly, *Modeling is Better Than Words*, heartlight.org, www.heartlight.org/articles/200011/20001114 wooden.html.

37. ESPN.com, *10 Burning Questions for John Wooden*, http://espn.go.com/page2/s/questions.wooden.html.

38. Wooden, John, Excerpt from *Wooden: A Lifetime of Observations and Reflections On and Off the Court*, www.coachjohn wooden.com.

39. ESPN.com, *10 Burning Questions for John Wooden*, http://espn.go.com/page2/s/questions.wooden.html .

40. Dahlberg, Tim, *Weir's diva attitude ruins chance for medal*, MSNBC.com, http://www.msnbc.msn.com/id/11397282/ .

41. Simon, Bob, *Bode*, cbsnews.com, http://www.cbsnews.com/stories/2006/01/05/60minutes/main1182654.shtml.

42. Greenberg, Jay, *A Golden Day for Team USA*, New York Post Online Edition, http://www.nypost.com/sports/59988.htm.

43. *Pride*, The American Heritage Dictionary of the English Language, Fourth Edition, Houghton Mifflin, New York, 2000.

44. Collins, Jim, *Good To Great: Why Some Companies Make the Leap...and Others Don't*, HarperBusiness, New York, 2001, 22.

45. Ibid.

46. Matthew 14:18–21, *The Holy Bible, New International Version (NIV)*, International Bible Society, Zondervan, Grand Rapids, 1984.

47. Matthew 14:14, *The Holy Bible, New International Version (NIV)*, International Bible Society, 1984.

48. Wooden, John, *Team Spirit*, Excerpt from *Wooden: A Lifetime of Observations and Reflections On and Off the Court*, Coach John Wooden Official Website, http://www.coach johnwooden.com

49. Steps in the 12 Step Program, *The 12 Steps*, http://www.12step.org/steps.

50. Ibid.

978-0-595-42787-1
0-595-42787-1

www.ingramcontent.com/pod-product-compliance
Lightning Source LLC
Chambersburg PA
CBHW030348290526
45785CB00004B/1649